ART NOUVEAU
Frames and Borders
250 Copyright-Free Illustrations
for Artists and Craftsmen

Edited by
Carol Belanger Grafton

Dover Publications, Inc.
New York

Copyright © 1983 by Dover Publications, Inc.
All rights reserved under Pan American and International Copyright Conventions.

Published in Canada by General Publishing Company, Ltd., 30 Lesmill Road, Don Mills, Toronto, Ontario.

Published in the United Kingdom by Constable and Company, Ltd., 10 Orange Street, London WC2H 7EG.

Art Nouveau Frames and Borders: 250 Copyright-Free Illustrations for Artists and Craftsmen is a new work, first published by Dover Publications, Inc., in 1983. The selection and arrangement of illustrations are by Carol Belanger Grafton. The research and Publisher's Note are by Joseph M. Cahn.

DOVER *Pictorial Archive* SERIES

Manufactured in the United States of America
Dover Publications, Inc., 180 Varick Street, New York, N.Y. 10014

Library of Congress Cataloging in Publication Data
Main entry under title:

Art nouveau frames and borders.

(Dover pictorial archive series)
1. Borders, Ornamental (Decorative arts) 2. Decoration and ornament—Art nouveau.
I. Grafton, Carol Belanger. II. Series.
NK3630.4.B67A78 1983   745.4   83-5219
ISBN 0-486-24513-6

PUBLISHER'S NOTE

The graphic invention of the Art Nouveau movement found some of its fullest expression in frames, borders and similar decorations in books, magazines and advertising. From about 1890 to about 1910, the infinitely varied curvilinear designs associated with such masters as Alphonse Maria Mucha (one of whose compositions appears on page 85) adorned the pages of many European and American publications. Though the movement was short-lived, its creative output was large and its influence far-reaching. Nearly a century after its first flowering, Art Nouveau is enjoying a lively revival among artists and craftspeople in many disciplines.

The sources of the design elements in the present collection are many and varied. Popular newspapers, literary magazines, trade journals and art periodicals in Dover's extensive archives yielded hundreds of frames and borders originally prepared as decorations in both editorial and advertising matter. Type specimen books also contributed material, mainly "piece borders" in several styles that were cast in units to be assembled by printers in various combinations and configurations. From this wealth of authentic period design, artist Carol Belanger Grafton has selected 250 of the most interesting and versatile graphics.

Serials searched include *The Inland Printer, St. Nicholas, The Strand Magazine, Windsor Magazine, Harmsworth Magazine, Life, Frank Leslie's Illustrated Newspaper, Harper's Weekly, The Studio, Art et Décoration, Über Land und Meer, The Youth's Companion* and *Simplicissimus.*

While much of the material in this collection is purely abstract, many of the frames and borders are composed of figurative elements, either in part or in full. Natural forms, especially plants and flowers, were among the most important sources of inspiration for Art Nouveau designers. This volume is appropriately rich in floral motifs. Some of them are traditional subjects of decoration, such as the acanthus leaves that have figured in architectural ornament since classical times. Others, such as the cascades of wisteria blossoms so evocative of Oriental splendor, were favorites of the *fin de siècle*. Stylized but recognizable images of flowers from every season, from the daffodils of early spring to the roses of summer, to autumnal chrysanthemums and even Christmas cactus, are arranged in wreaths and garlands.

Other figurative elements add variety, interest and widely adaptable symbolism to the frames and borders assembled here. The animal kingdom contributes cats, lions, dolphins, mice, turtles, owls, dragonflies and, of course peacocks, the very emblem of the Art Nouveau style. Human figures appear here and there, particularly doe-eyed women with flowing hair, whose tresses are often worked into the supporting frames. There are cherubs and mermaids as well, and, at the top of page 75, Icarus strains toward heaven. Images of music, fine arts and printing trades suggest many potential uses. There are hints of exotic influences: rampant dragons at the bottom of page 35 have a Far Eastern flavor; papyrus and pomegranates on the upper right of page 43 evoke the mystery of ancient Egypt.

Advertisers, designers and illustrators will appreciate the diversity of shapes presented here—square, oblong, round, oval and heart-shaped frames. There is one in the shape of an ornate hand-mirror decorated with the inevitable peacock feathers, and there are others whose forms defy description. Many have the eye-catching asymmetry so beloved of turn-of-the-century designers, and nearly all have the serpentine fluidity that can add life to the simplest typography. The frames and borders range in size from cartouches suitable for enclosing a small ad to elaborate, full-page compositions that might dress up a menu or flyer. Some are delicate, open-work arrangements of tracery; others are bold and massive. Some are showpieces of the engraver's art, with fine hatching and stippling, but all are printed in clear line for ready reproduction.

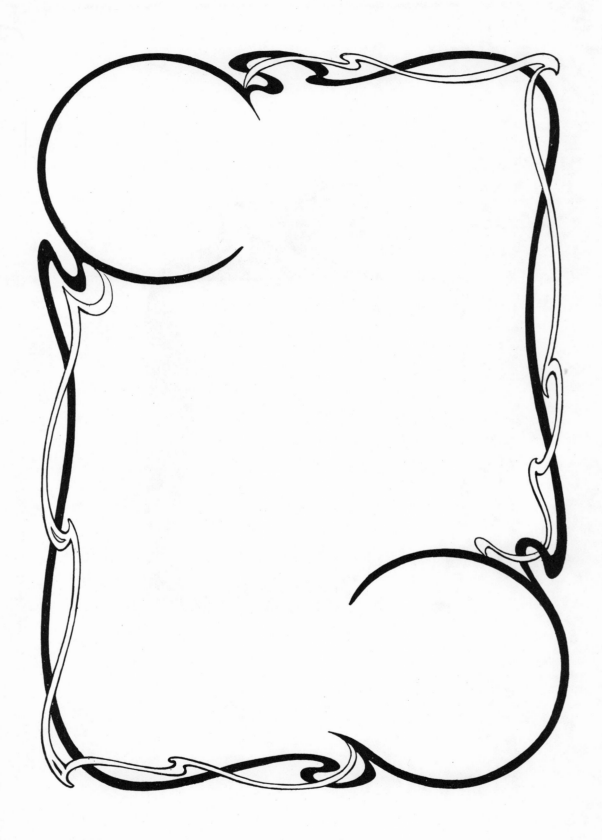

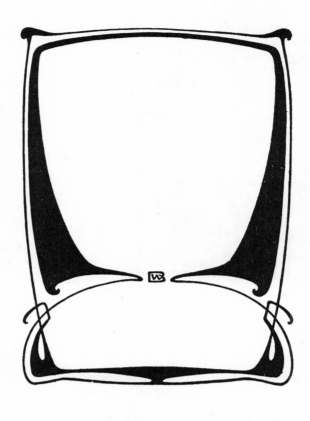

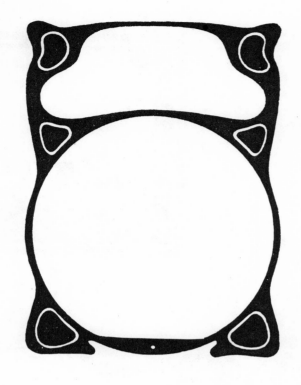

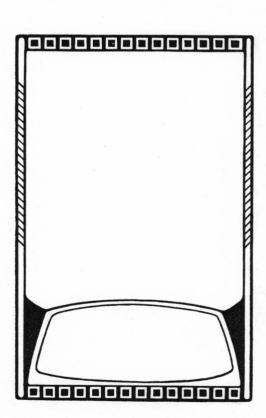

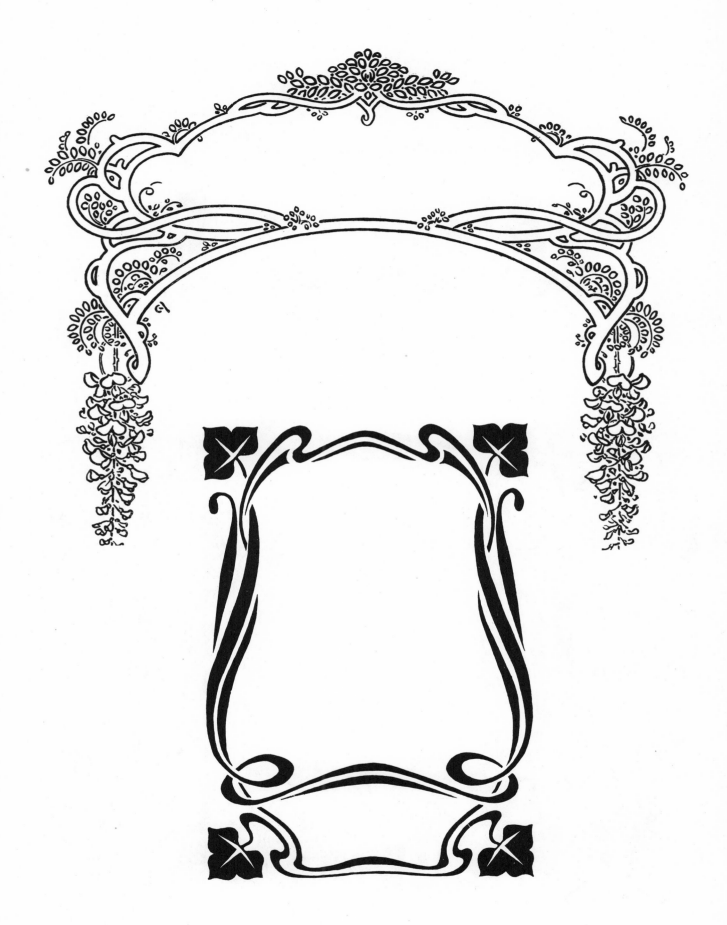

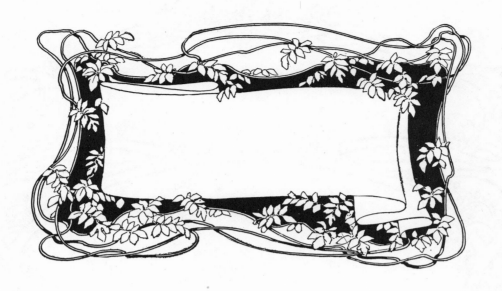

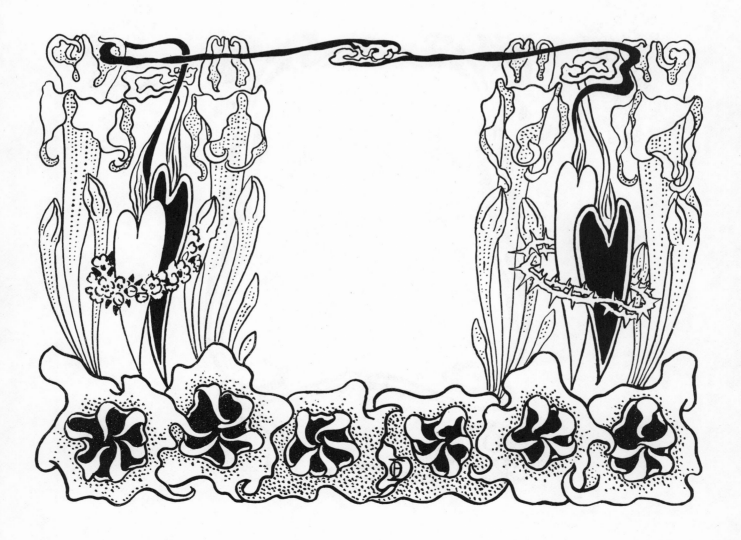

10

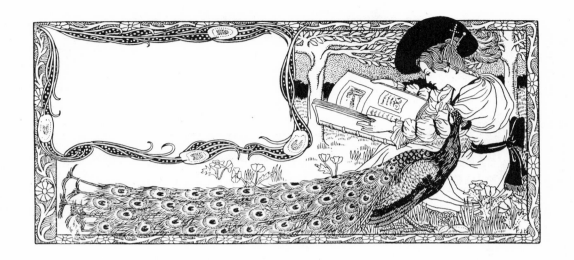

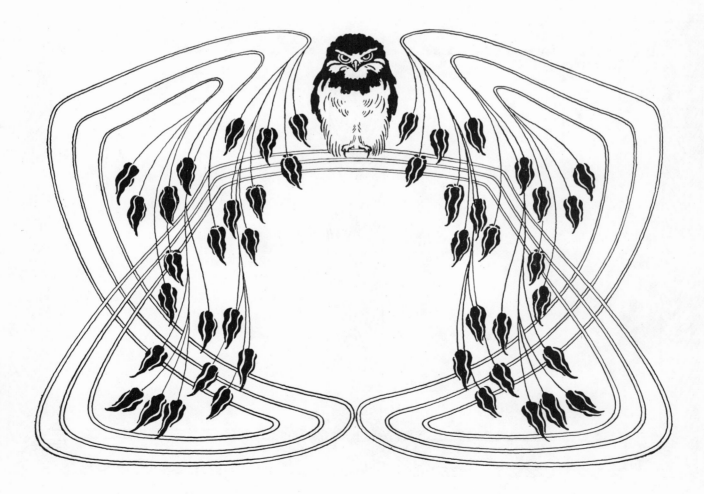

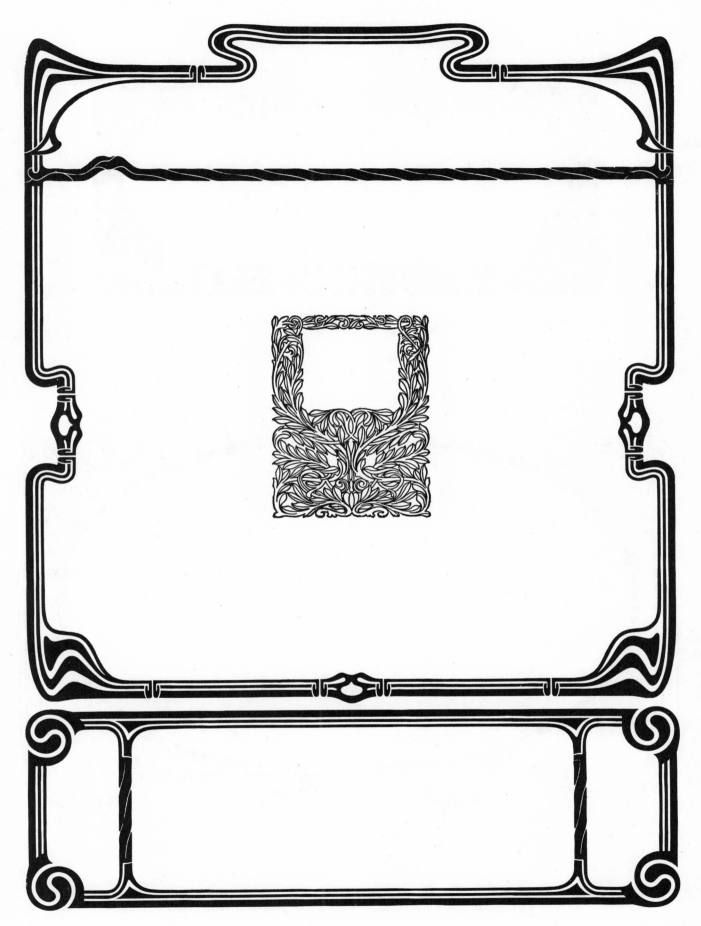

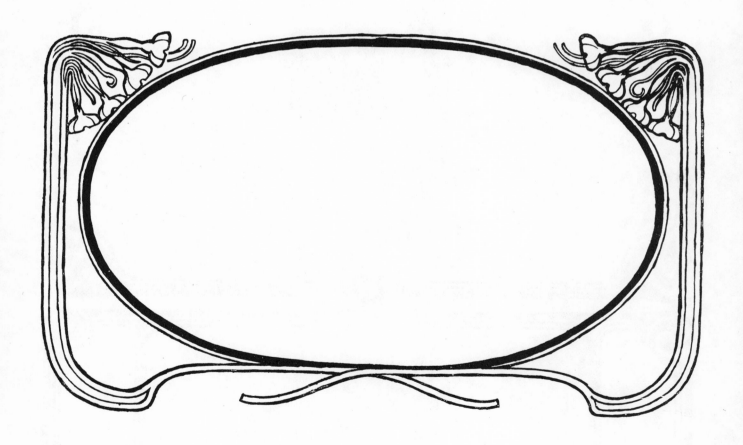

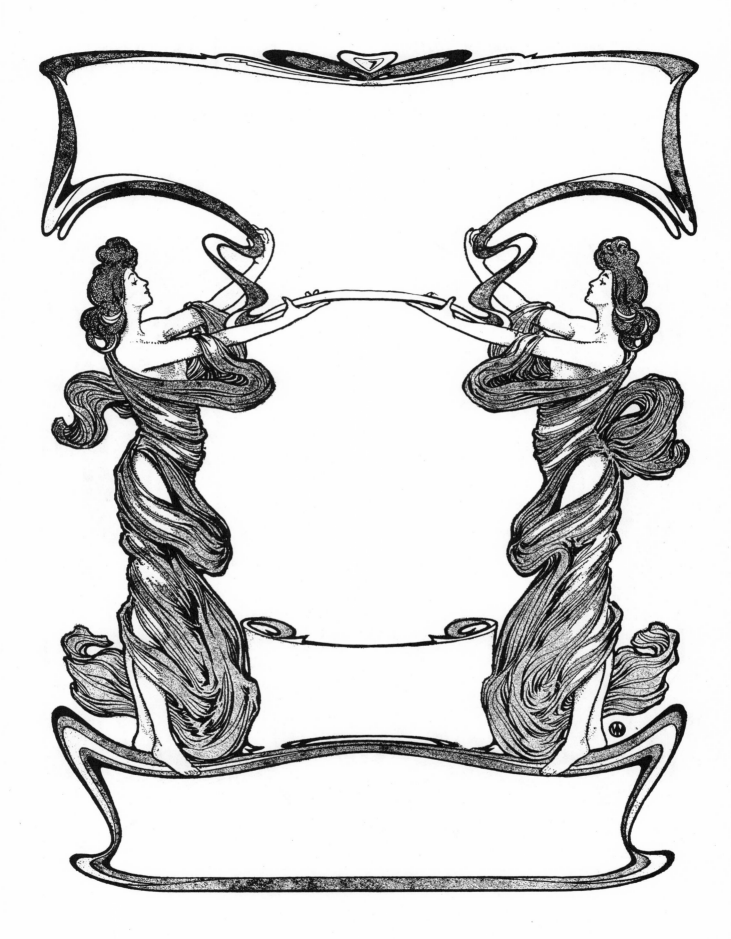

17

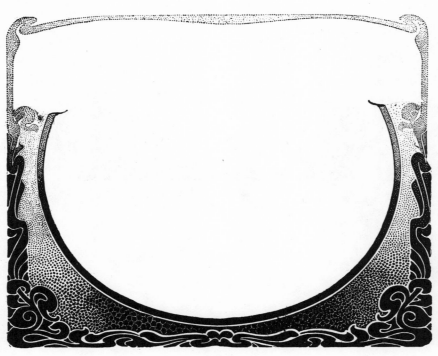

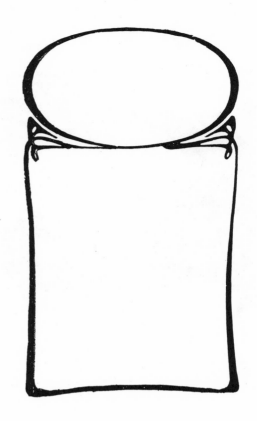

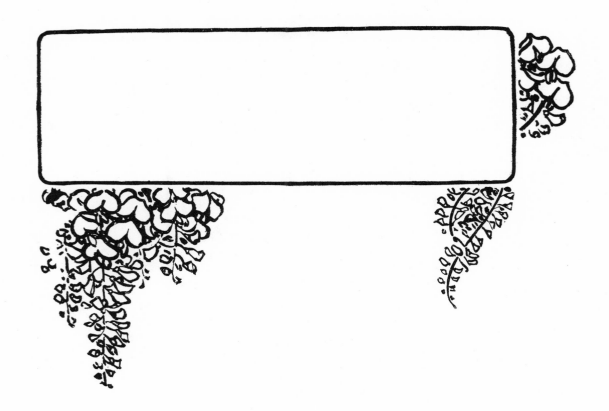

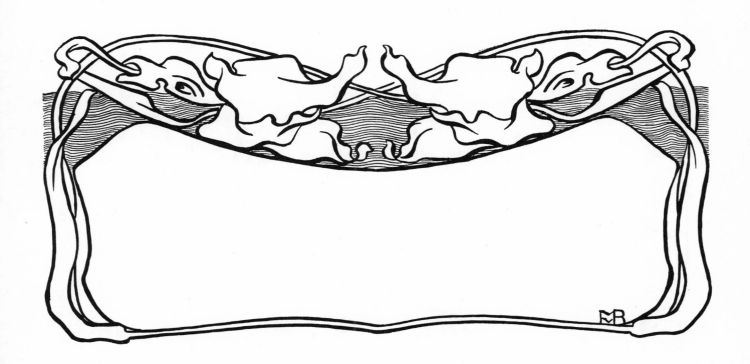

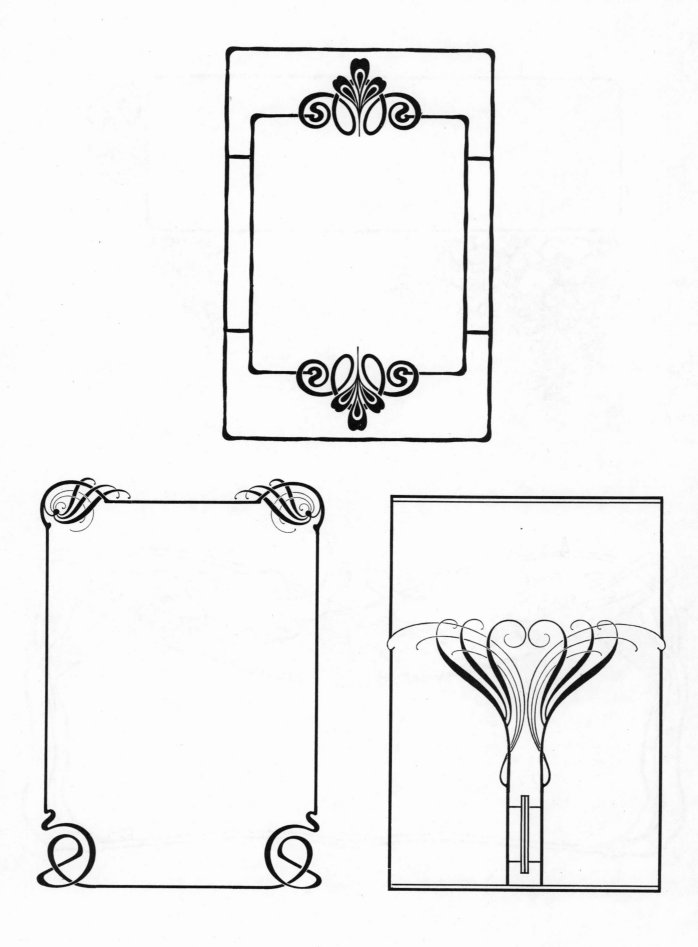

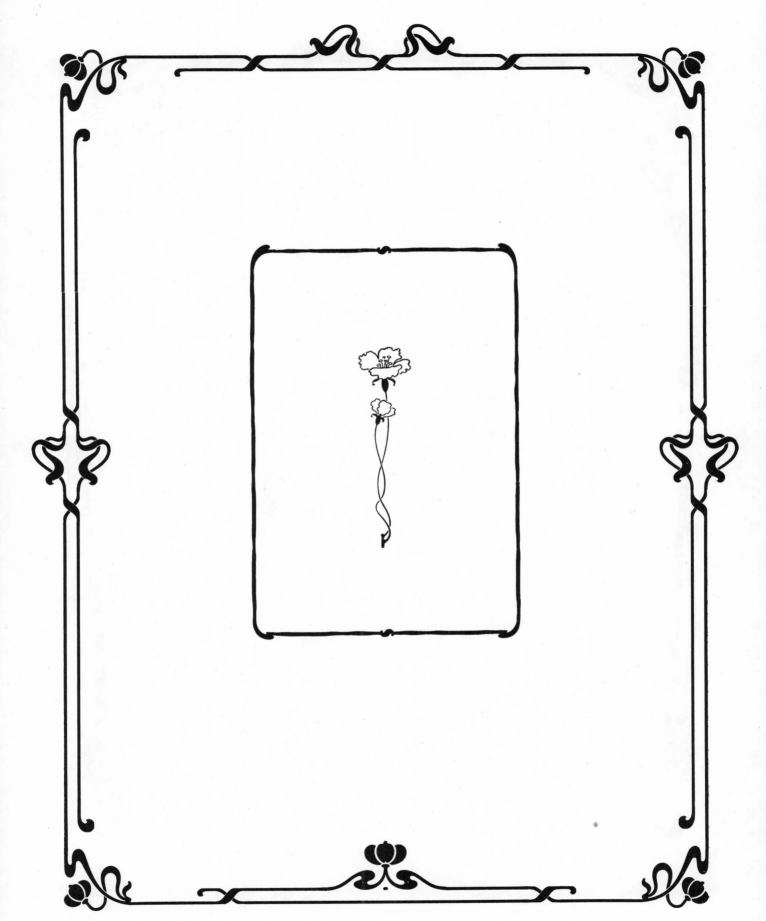

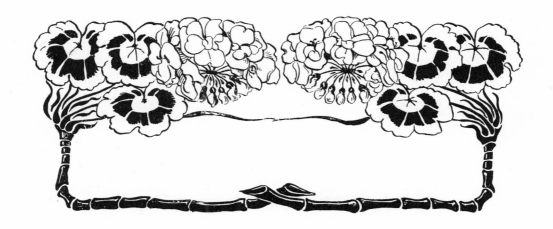

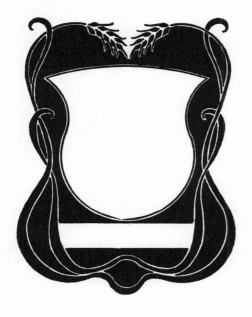

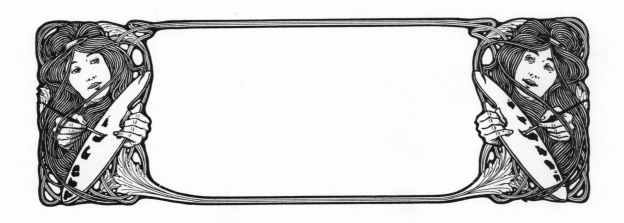

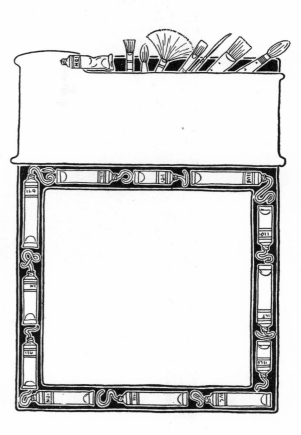

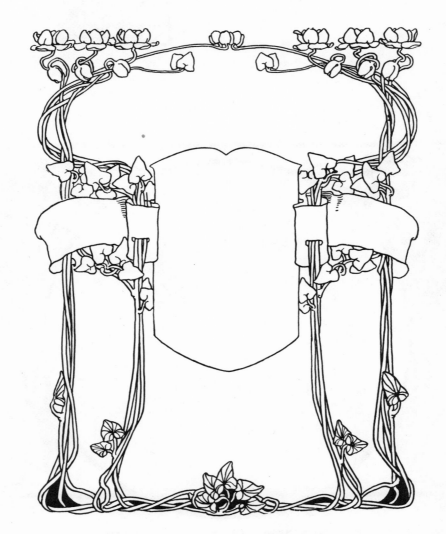

Ex-Libris

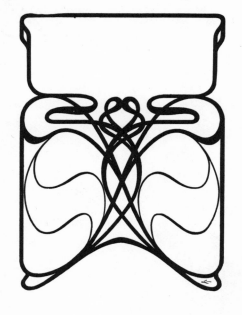

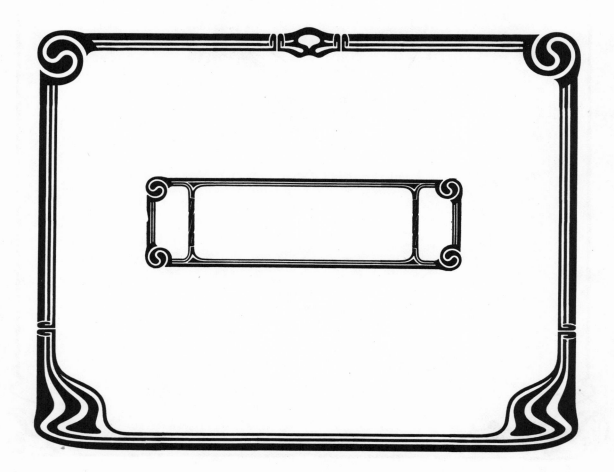

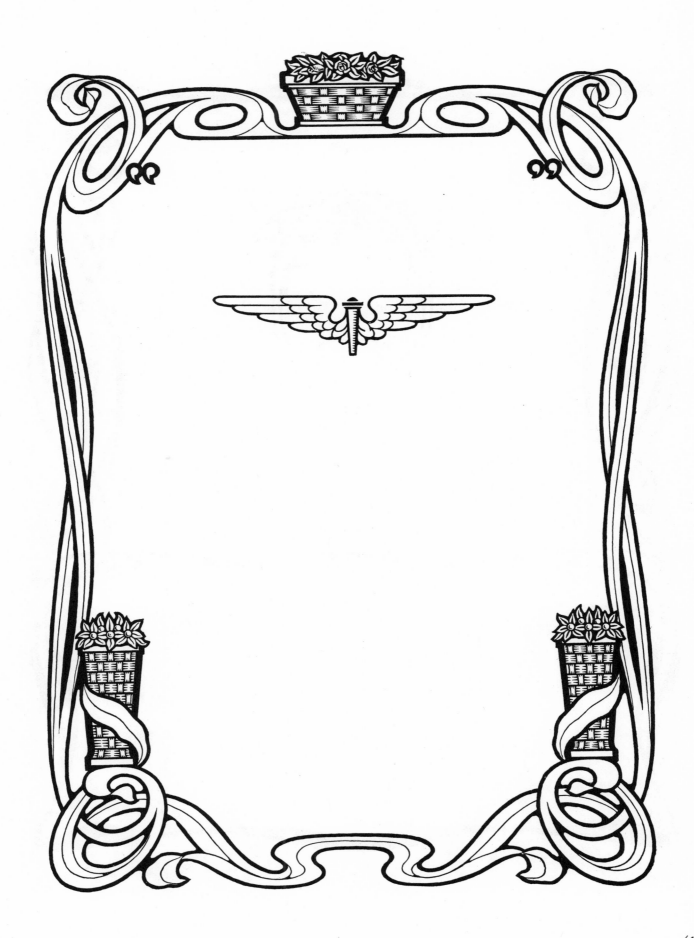

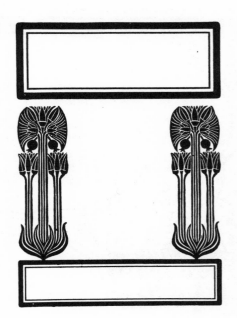

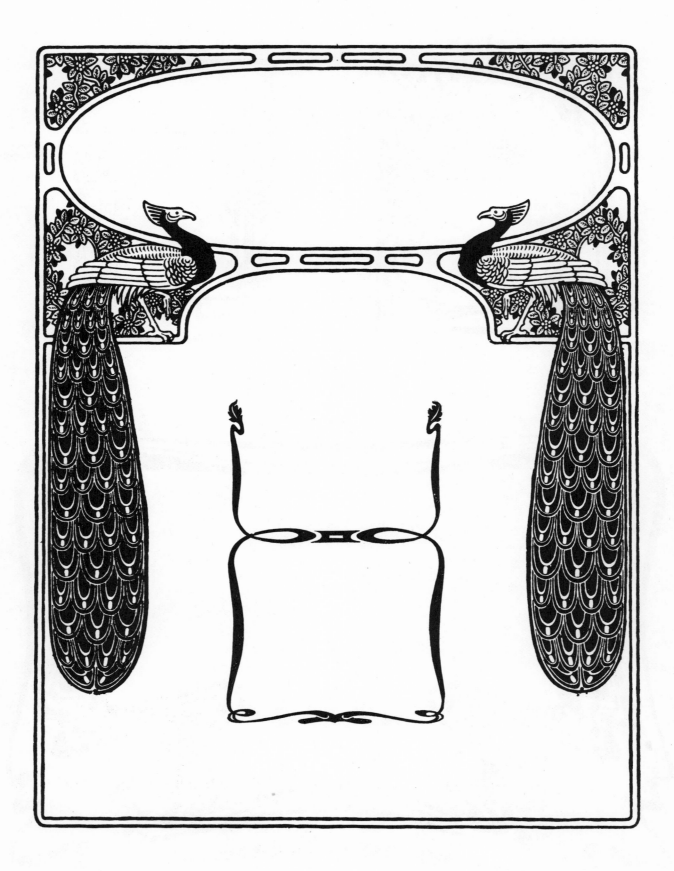

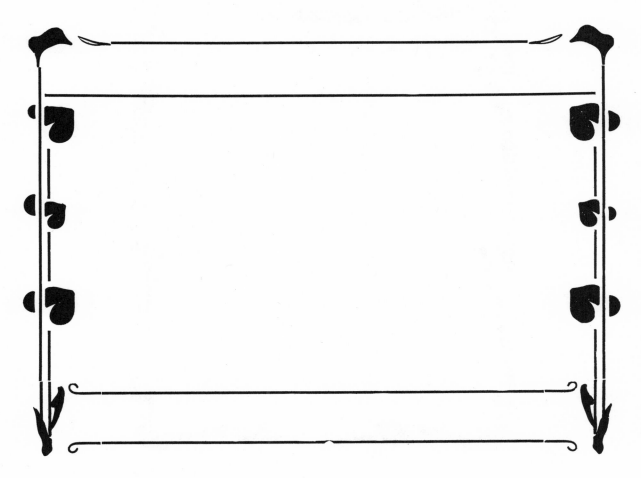

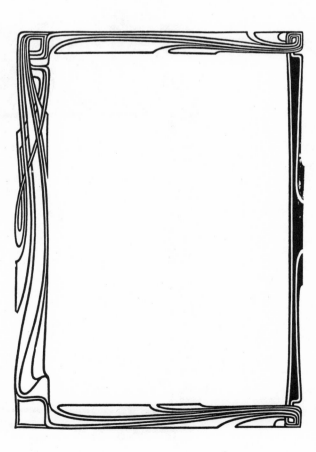

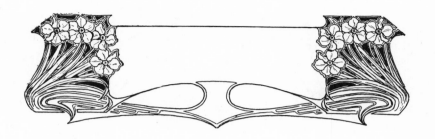

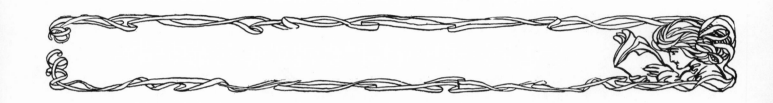

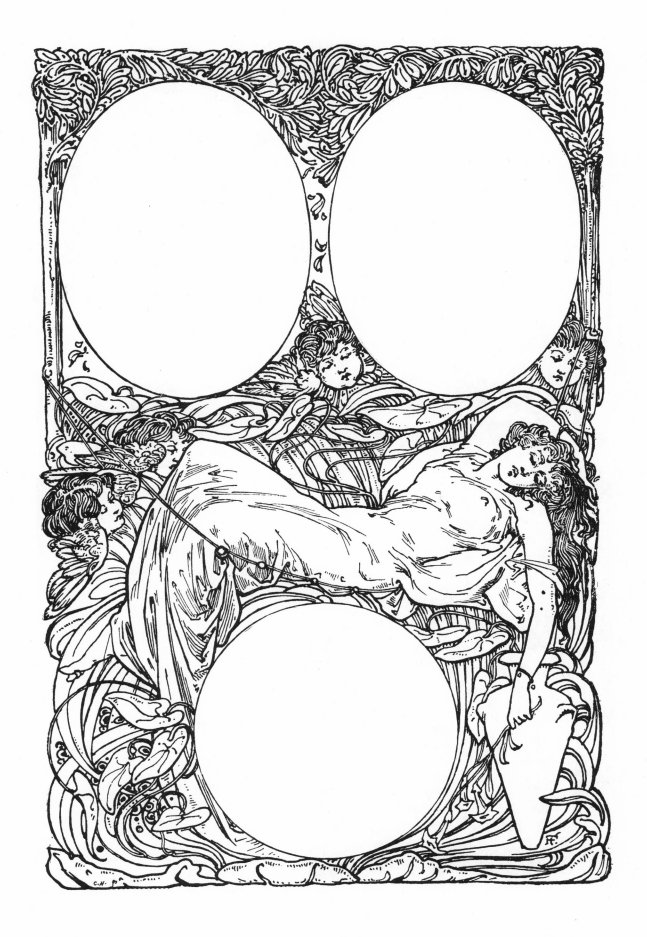

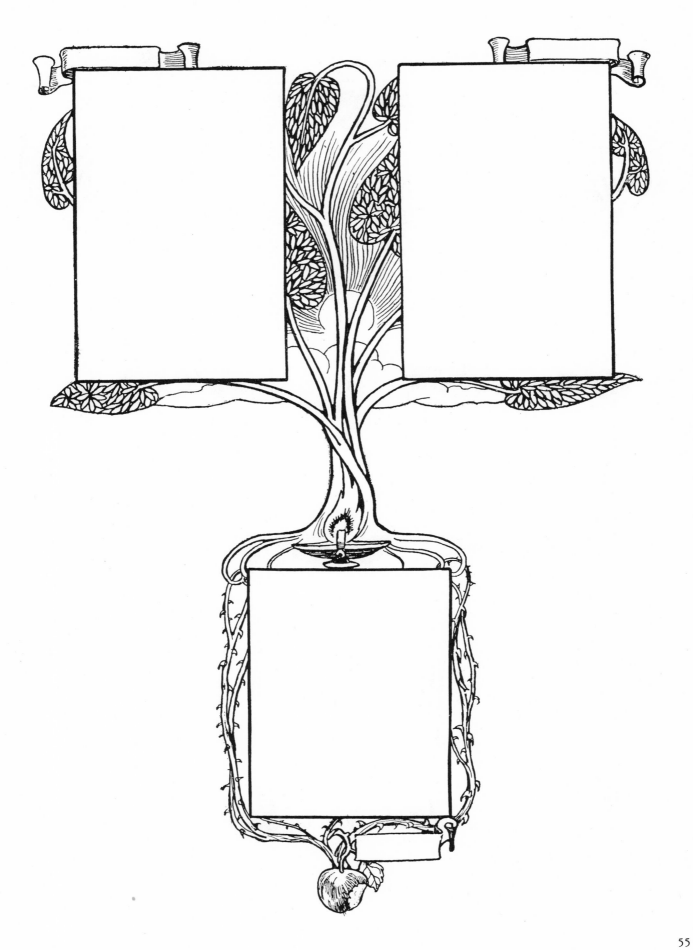

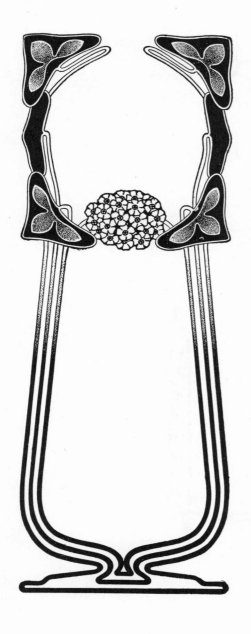

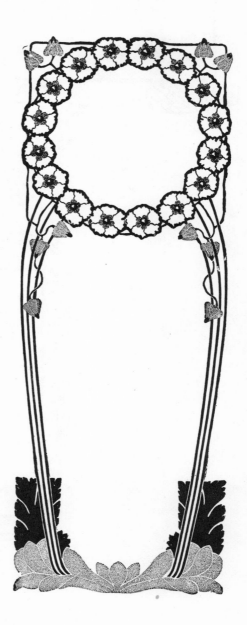

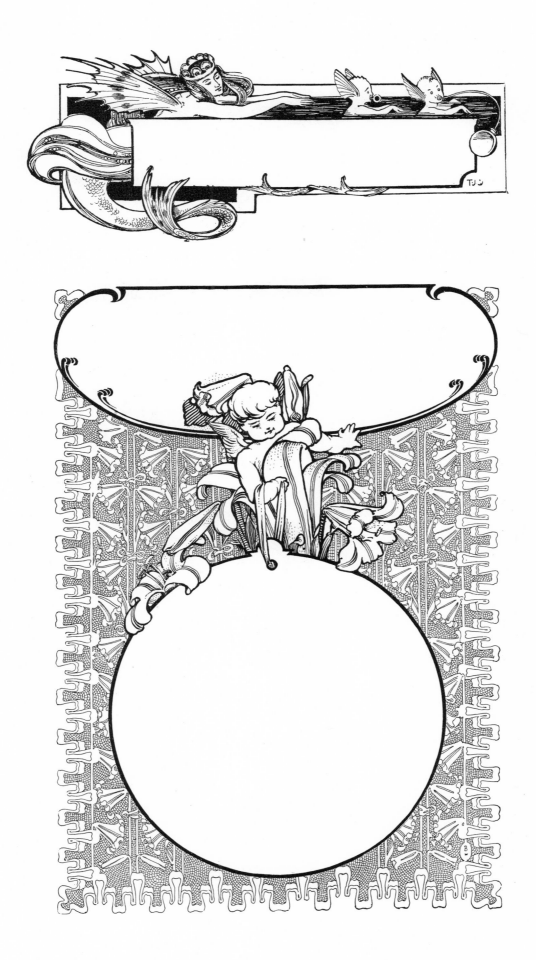

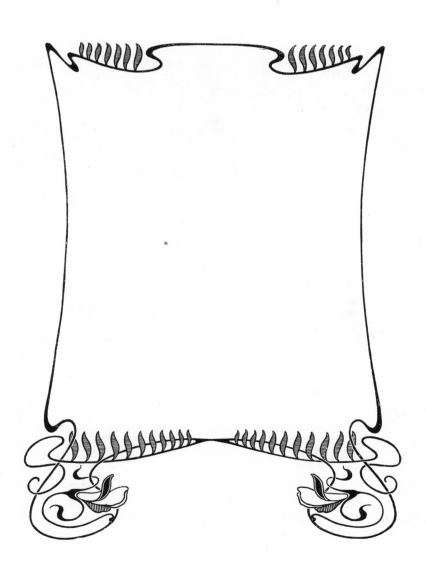

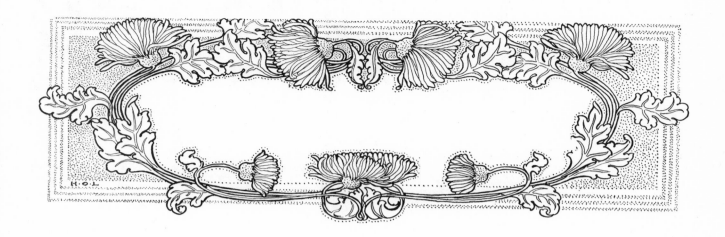

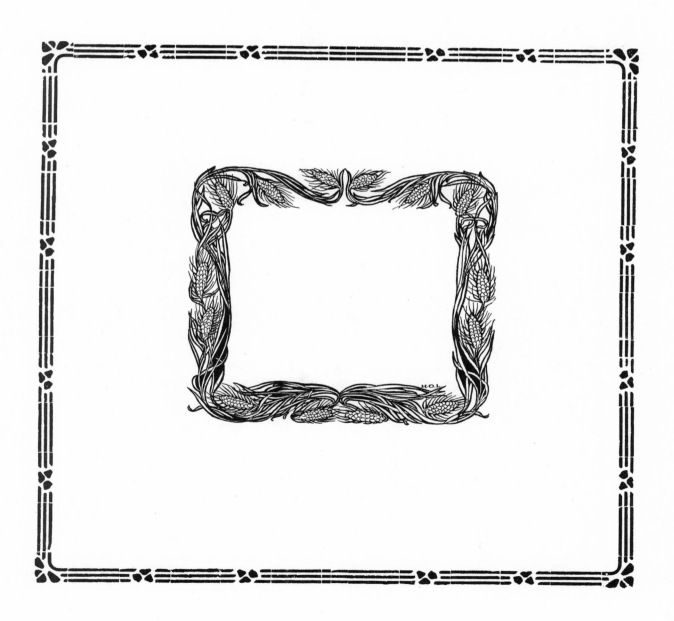

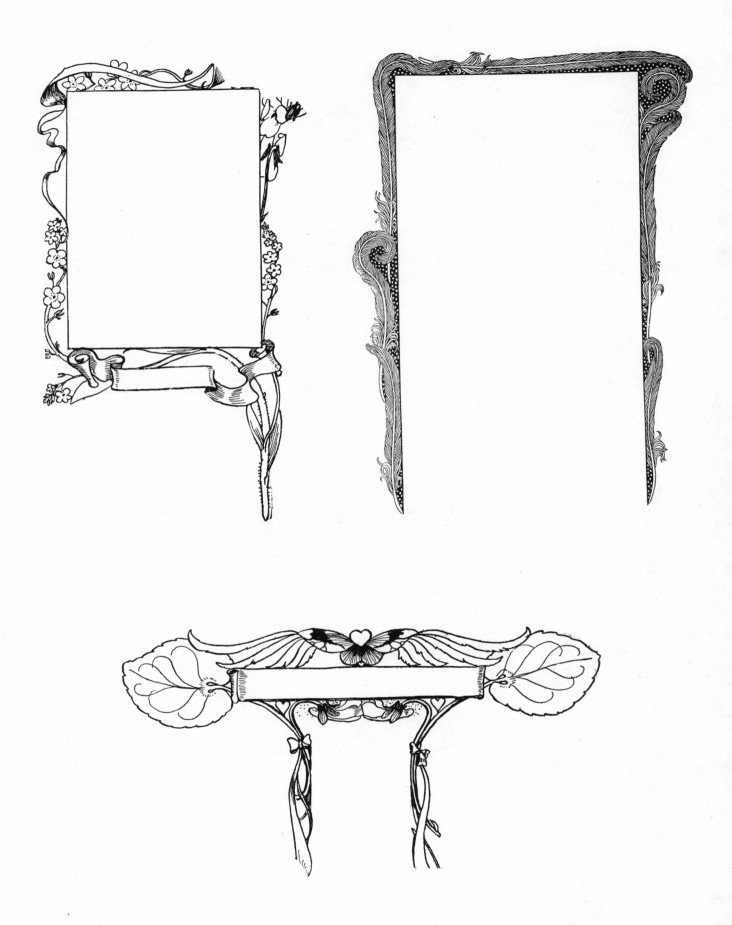

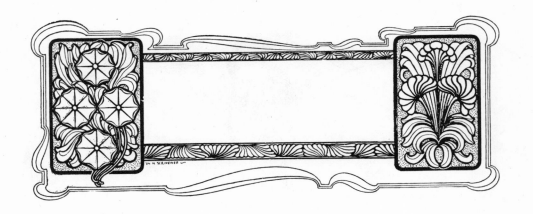

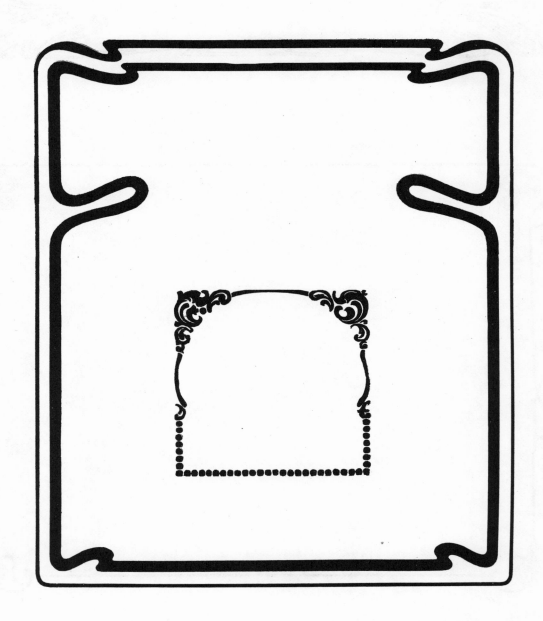

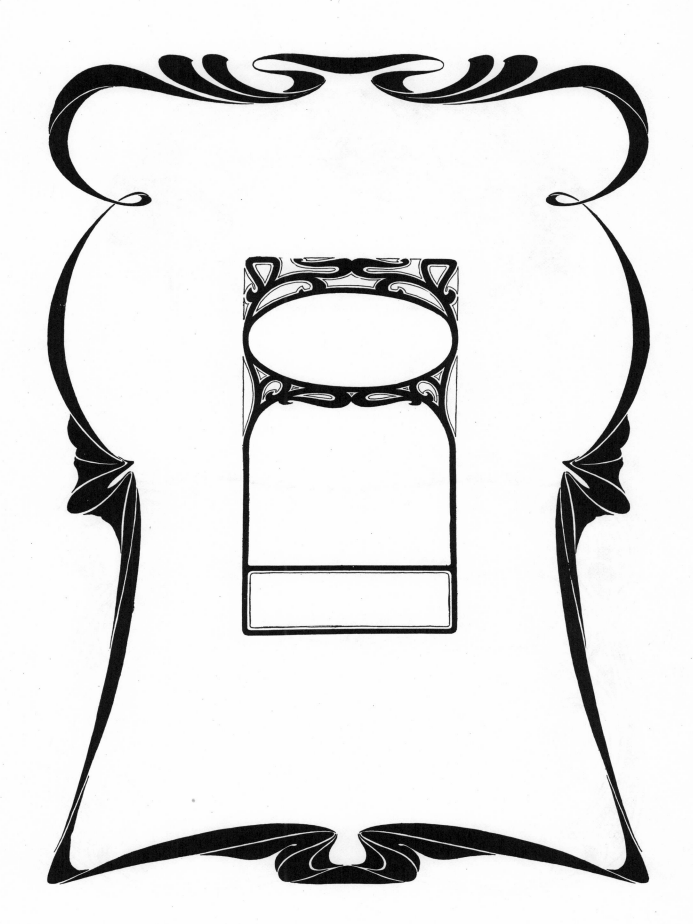

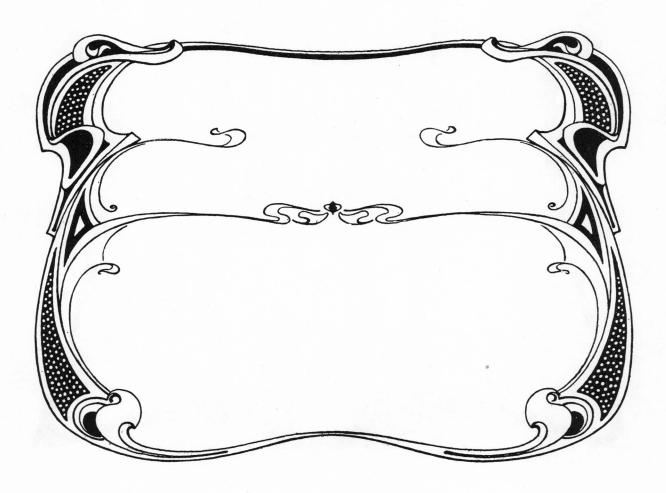

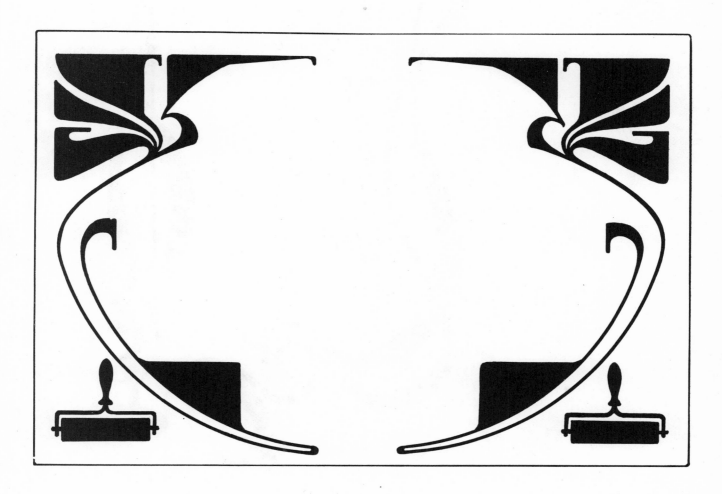

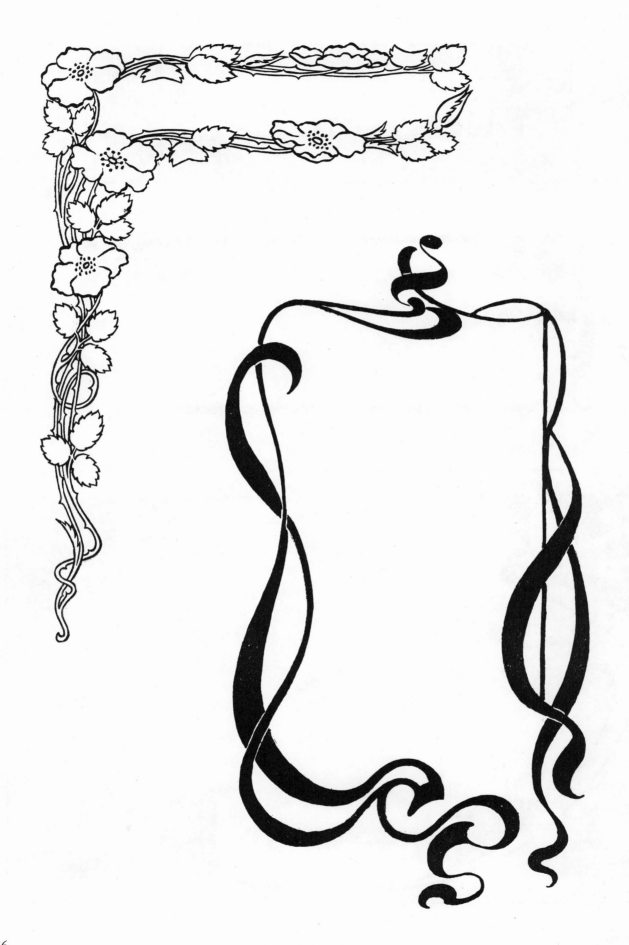

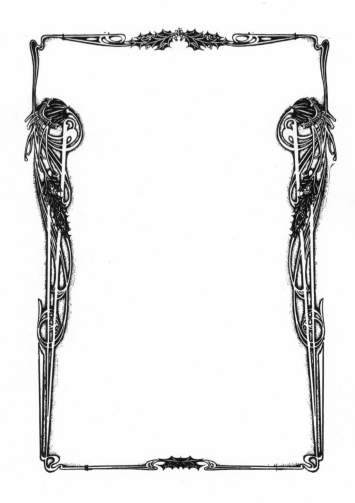

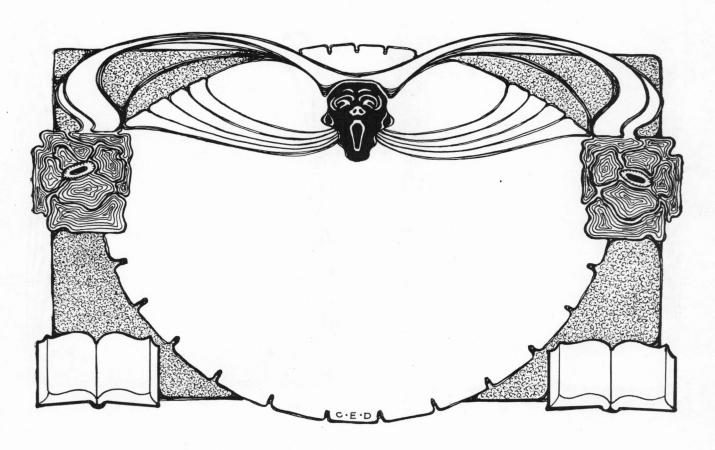

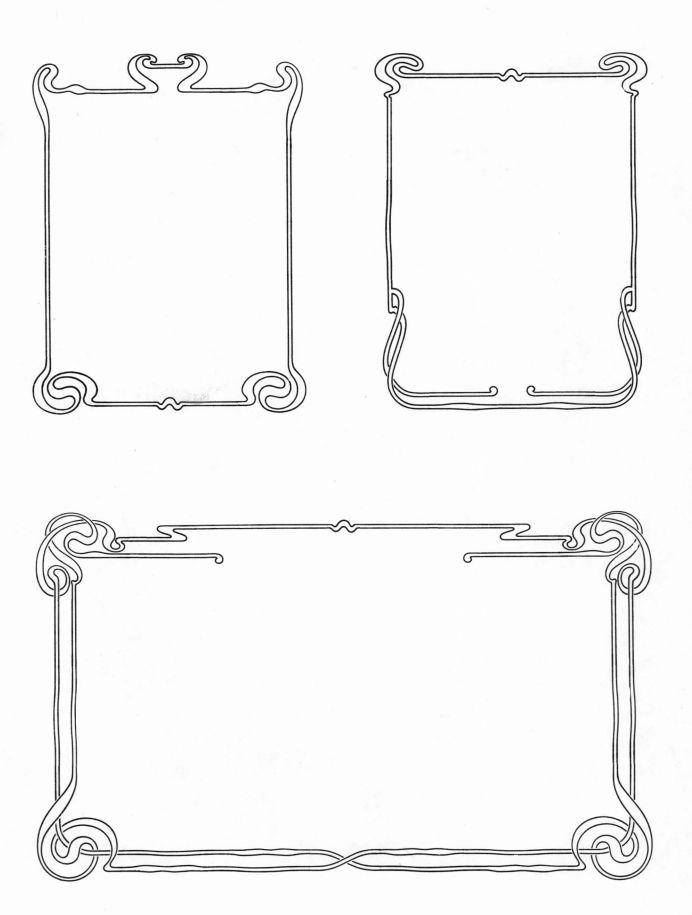

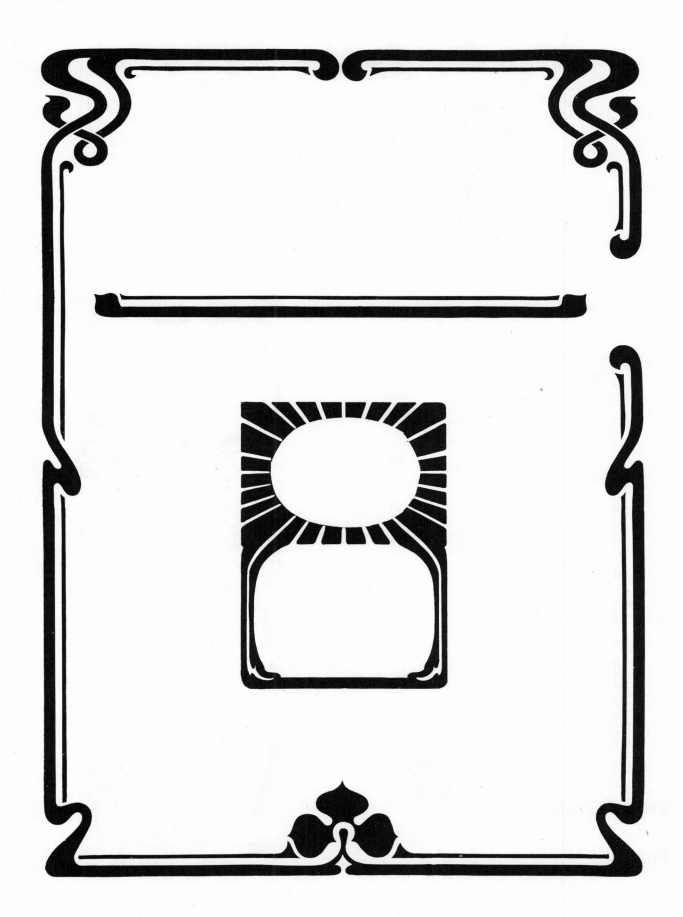

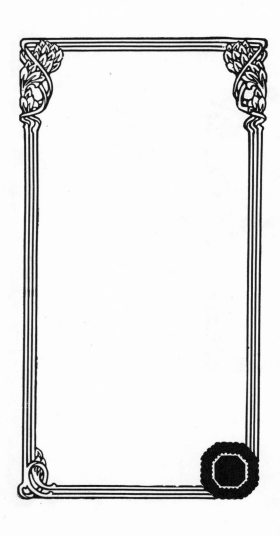

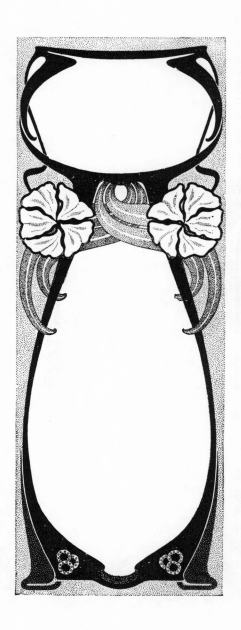

84

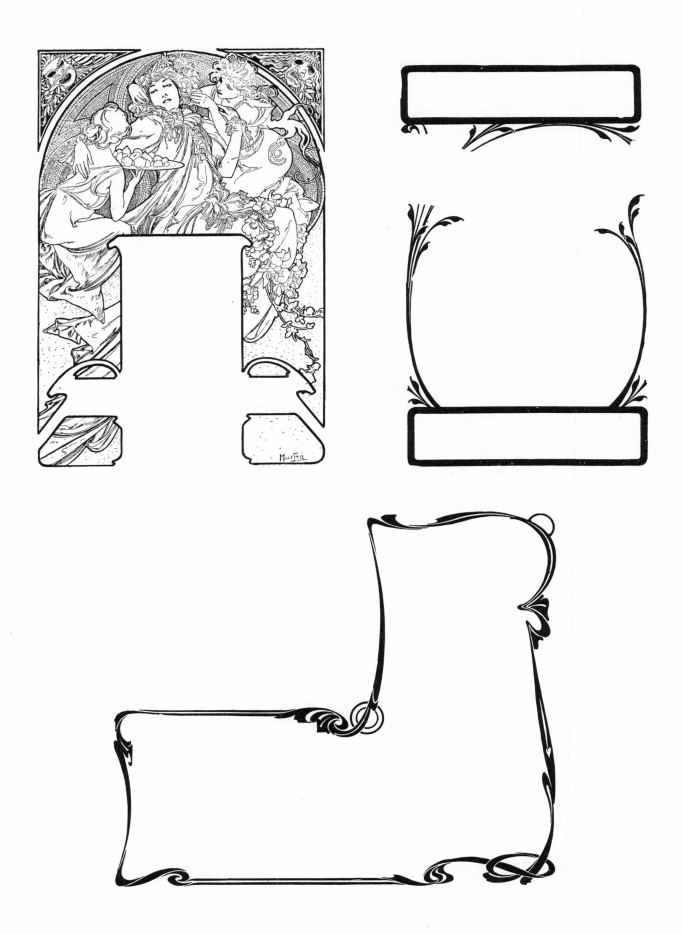

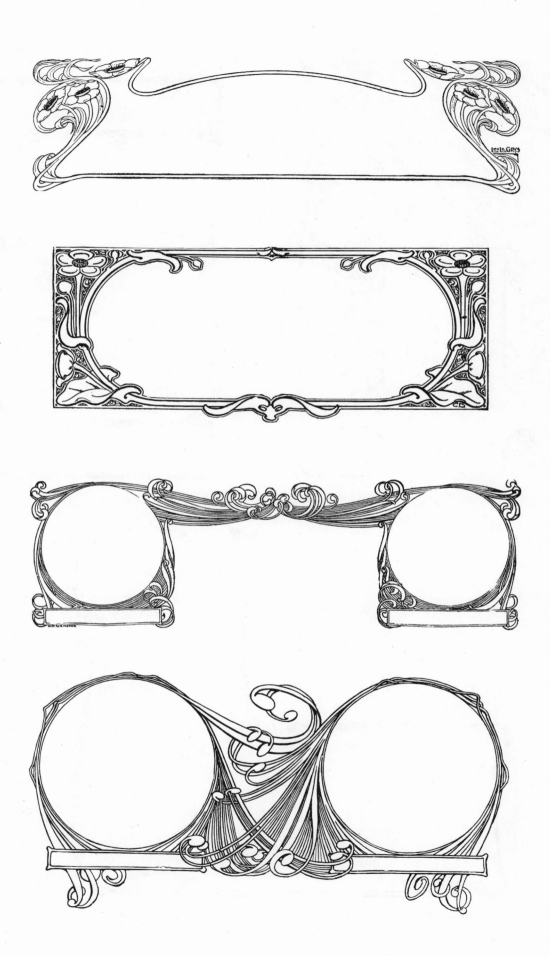

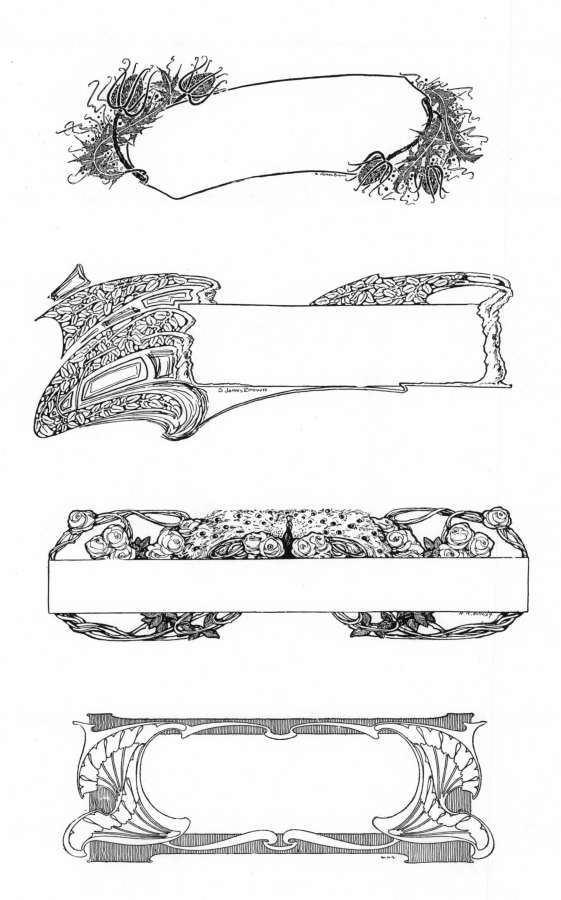

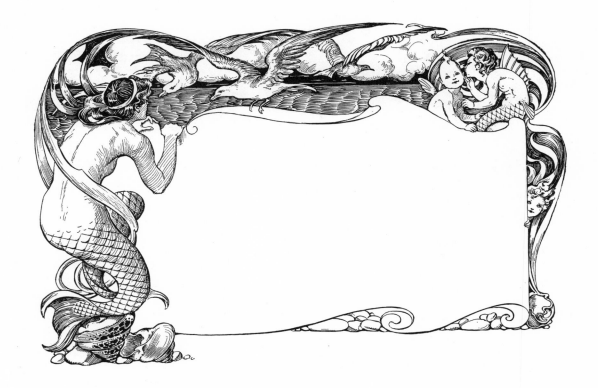

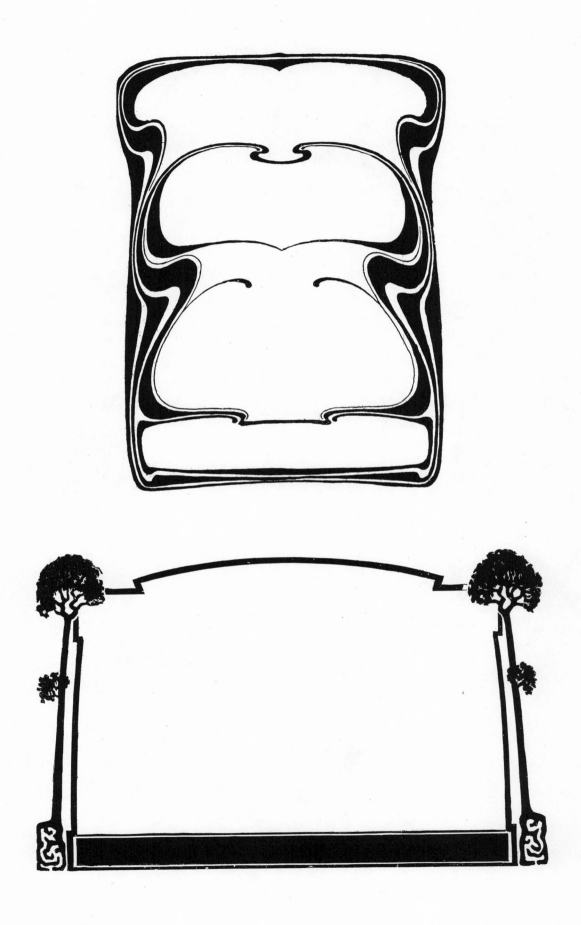

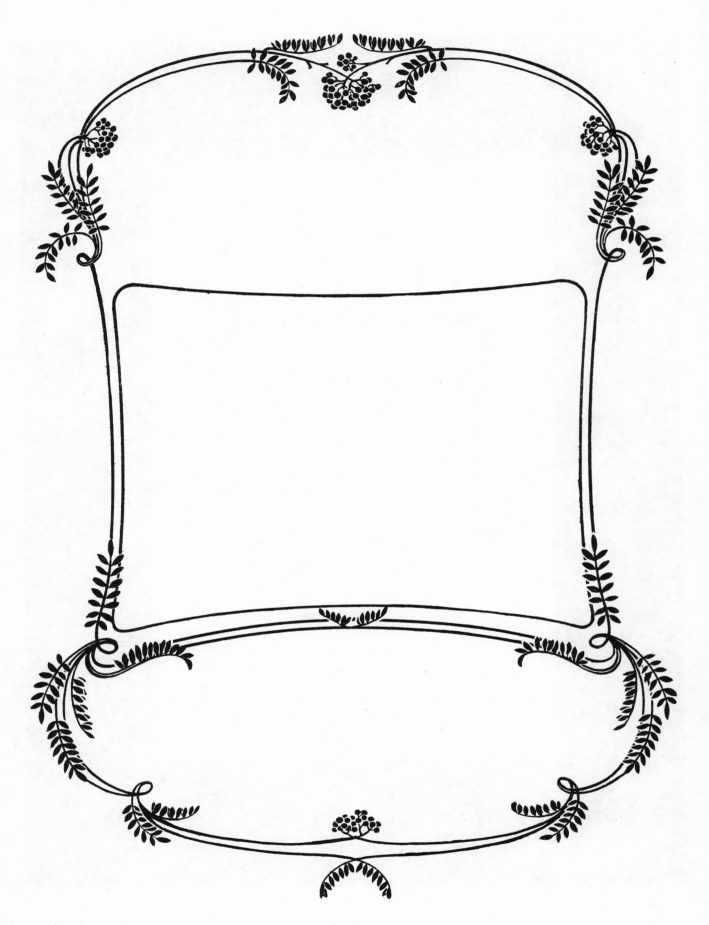

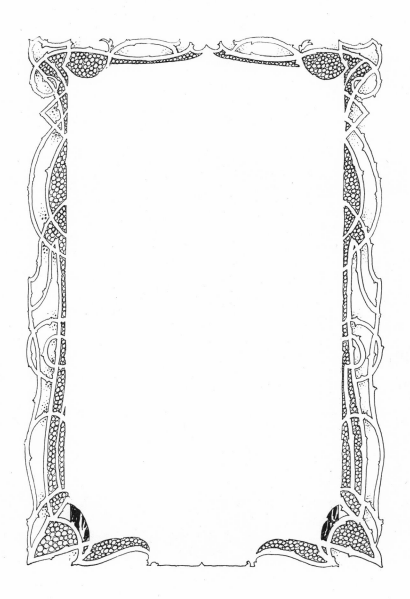

101

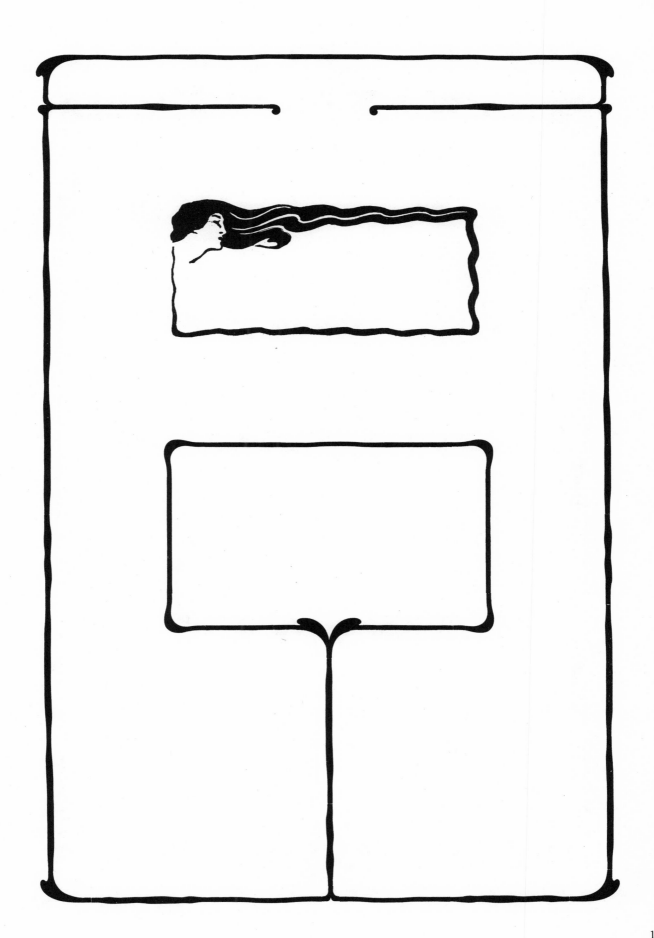

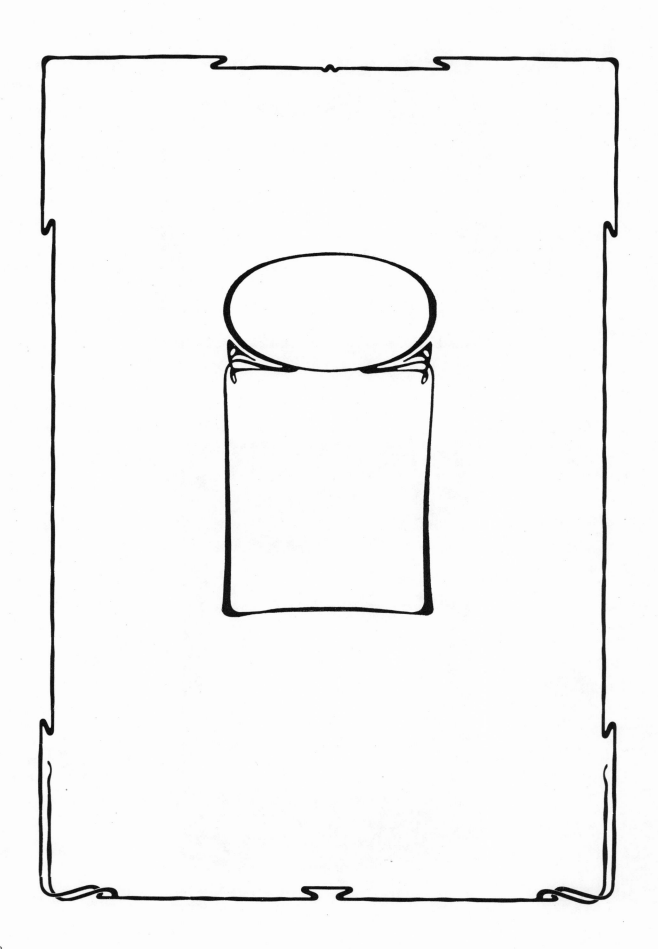

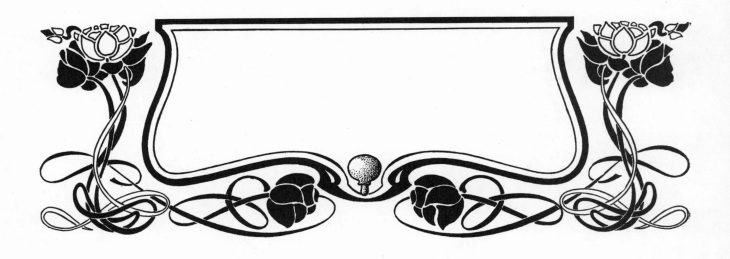

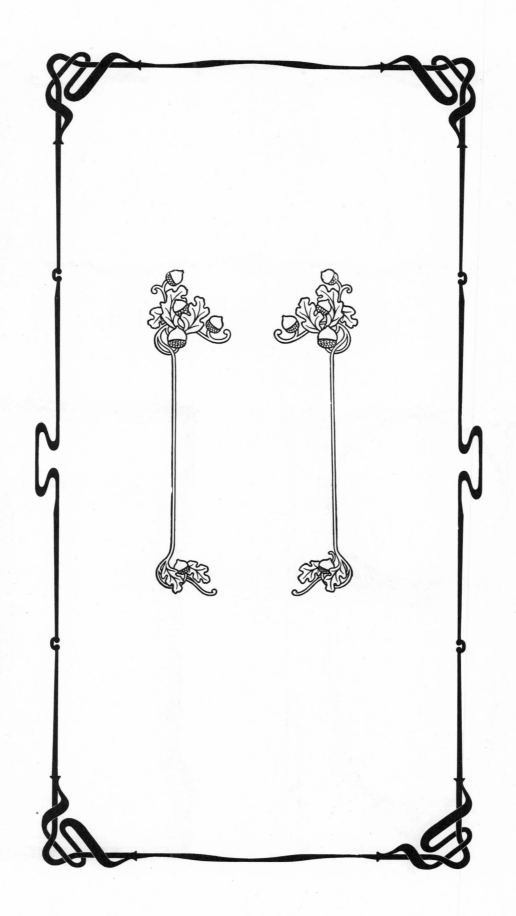

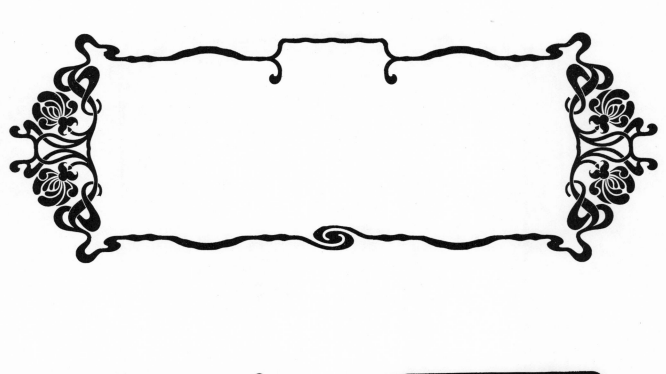

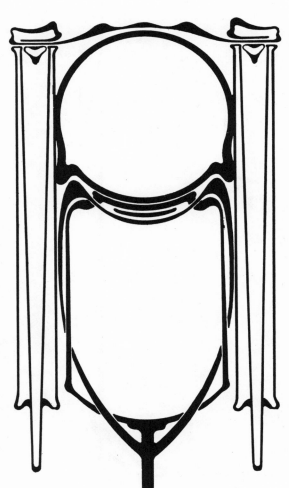

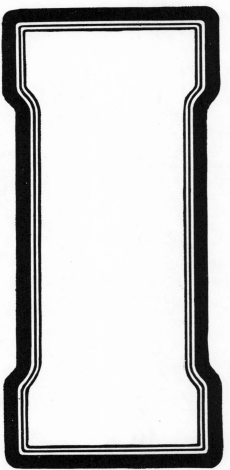

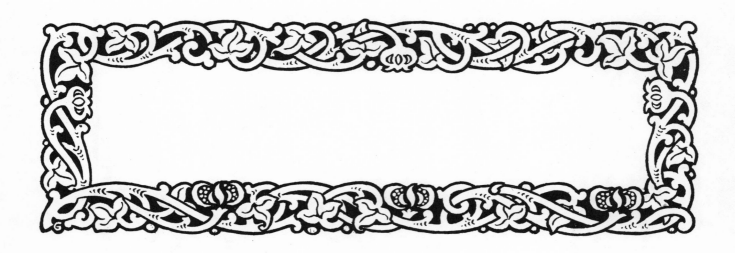

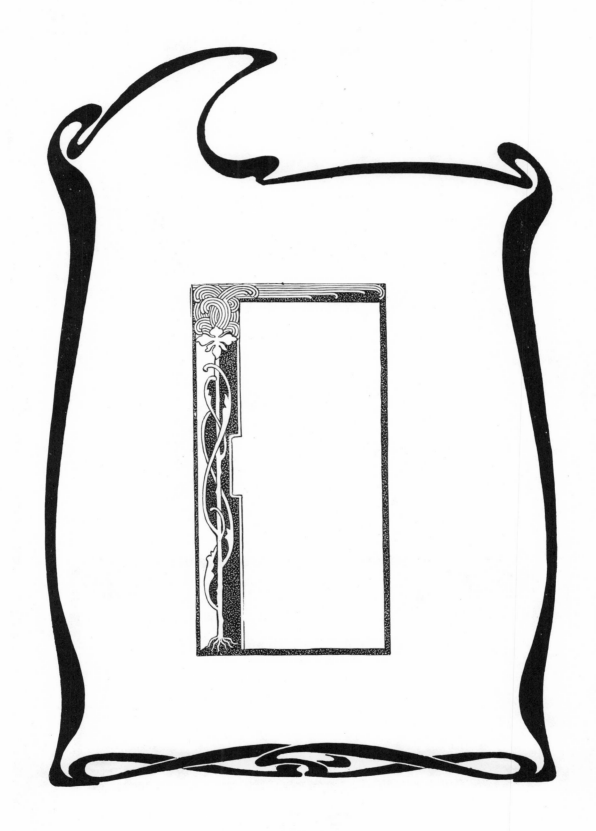

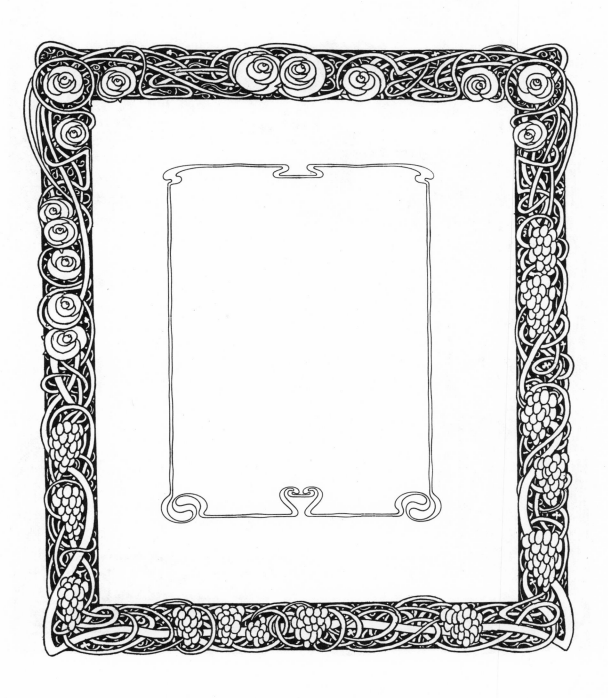

119

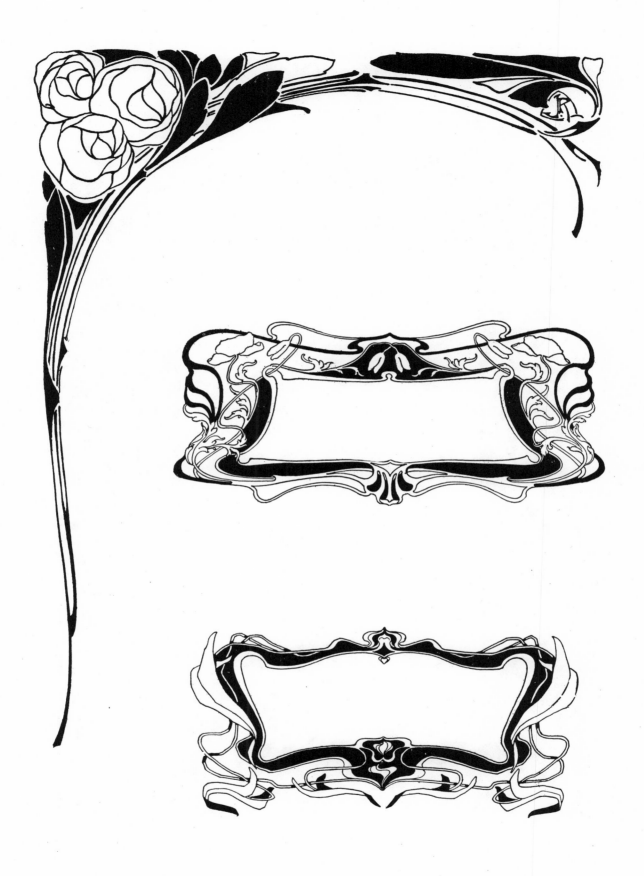